GW00771818

Michel Thomas

SPANISH
LANGUAGE
BUILDER

Hodder & Stoughton

A MEMBER OF THE HODDER HEADLINE GROUP

Press reviews for *Michel Thomas Language Courses*

The Times
'the nearest thing to painless learning'

The Daily Telegraph
'works like a dream'

Sunday Business
'…ideal for any business traveller who needs to be able to get around confidently'

Time Out
'…five minutes into the first CD, you already feel like you're winning'

Red
'Hugely inspiring'

Daily Star
'Michel's methods will teach you effectively and easily'

The Daily Telegraph
'a great way to learn; it's fast and it lasts'

First published in UK 2001 by Hodder Headline Ltd, 338 Euston Road, London NW1 3BH.

Typeset by Transet Limited, Coventry, England.
Printed in Great Britain by Circle Services Ltd, Southend-on-Sea, Essex

Introduction

Who is Michel Thomas?

Michel Thomas is head of the Michel Thomas Language Centers and has been teaching languages for over fifty years, primarily in New York, Beverly Hills, and London. He is a graduate of the Department of Philology at the University of Bordeaux, France, and has studied psychology at the Sorbonne (Paris) and at the University of Vienna. However, it is his remarkable life experiences that have fuelled his passion for teaching languages*.

Michel spent most of his childhood in Germany and France. With the rise of Hitler, he began his years of escape and resistance. He spent two brutal years in French concentration and slave labour camps, constantly threatened by deportation to German death camps. He escaped and fought for the French Resistance, surviving capture, interrogation and torture.

Michel's wartime experiences, particularly his torture by the Gestapo when he discovered the ability to block out pain, made Michel Thomas aware of the untapped potential of the human mind. However, it was his deeply held conviction that the biggest weapon in maintaining a free society was education that drove him to devote his life to probing the learning process. Michel moved to Los Angeles in 1947, and he set up a language institute in Beverly Hills. Over a period of fifty years, he has developed a unique and revolutionary learning system that has made him the world's leading language teacher.

*For a full account of his fascinating life, read 'The Test of Courage: Michel Thomas' by Christopher Robbins, published by Random House

What is the Michel Thomas method?

Over a period of fifty years, Michel Thomas has developed and perfected a unique method of teaching languages**. In essence, he breaks a language down to its component parts and enables learners to reconstruct the language themselves to form their own sentences, to say what they want, when they want. The experience of learning a language becomes so exciting and satisfying that it stimulates self-motivation and builds confidence.

Who is the *Spanish Language Builder* for?
People who have already learned Spanish with Michel Thomas

The *Language Builder* does just what its name suggests: it builds on the language Michel teaches in his 8-hour course. It does this in two important and inseparable ways: by echoing the 8-hour course to review key structures, while at the same time presenting new idioms (which are heard and used all the time in everyday Spanish but which are very rarely taught). This dual approach means that you painlessly review what you have learned as you simultaneously expand the range of your working and functional knowledge of the language.

People who have learned Spanish using other methods

You may have learned Spanish before and now want to brush it up for a holiday or business trip, or perhaps you are looking for a new approach to help with revision or to re-motivate you, either way, the *Language Builder* will give you a real insight into how the language works and will boost your confidence to speak.

You may find that it takes a while to get used to Michel's innovative way of teaching – it is certainly quite unlike any other method you will have come across – but once you have experienced the excitement of painless learning you will be hooked!

**U.S. patent pending. All rights reserved

2

What does the pack contain?

The pack comprises approximately two hours of recorded material plus a 40-page booklet. The recordings are available on CD or audio cassette and feature Michel Thomas alone. To avoid wasting recording time, there are no pauses on the recordings, but you are strongly recommended to use the pause button on your player for maximum learning (see below). The booklet contains the key words and phrases to help you with written Spanish, but you do not need to use it at all if you just want to concentrate on improving your speaking and listening skills.

How do I use the recordings?

● Relax!

As far as possible, make yourself comfortable before playing the recordings and try to let go of the tensions and anxieties traditionally associated with all learning.

● Interact fully with the recordings

Use the pause button to stop the recording so that you have time to think out your translations. Then say the phrase or sentence out loud (or in a whisper, or in your head, if you are in a public place), before Michel does. This is essential. You do not learn by repetition but by thinking out the sentences yourself; it is by your own thought process that you truly learn.

● Stop the recording whenever it suits you

You will notice that the recordings are not divided into lessons*** so it is easy to stop wherever you want.

*****Tracking breaks have been inserted on the CDs: you may find it helpful to make a note of these (or the timings, if you have audio cassettes) in this booklet to help you get back immediately to where you left off or to review specific points*

What level of language will I achieve?

The recordings will give you a practical and functional use of the spoken language. Michel Thomas teaches the everyday conversational language that will allow you to communicate in a wide variety of situations, empowered by the ability to create your own sentences and use the language naturally.

How can I go on to improve further?

Obviously, nothing compares with first-hand contact with native Spanish speakers, but if this is not possible for you, Michel recommends reading Spanish newspapers and magazines as one of the best ways to keep up and extend your language. Interviews are particularly good, as they reflect Spanish as it is actually being spoken, rather than the language taught in schools or textbooks.

Who has Michel Thomas taught?

People travel from all over the world to learn a foreign language with Michel Thomas – because his method works. His students, now numbering in the thousands, have included well-known people from the arts and from the corporate, political and academic worlds. Michel's list of clients include:

● *Celebrities*: Mel Gibson, Emma Thompson, Woody Allen, Barbra Streisand, Warren Beatty, Melanie Griffith, Eddie Izzard, Bob Dylan, Jean Muir, Donald Sutherland, Jane Fonda, Anne Bancroft, Mel Brooks, Nastassja Kinski, Carl Reiner, Raquel Welch, Johnny Carson, Julie Andrews, Isabelle Adjani, Candice Bergen, Barbara Hershey, Priscilla Presley, Loretta Swit, Tony Curtis, Diana Ross, Herb Alpert, Angie Dickinson, Lucille Ball, Doris Day, Janet Leigh, Natalie Wood, Jayne Mansfield, Ann-Margaret, Yves Montand, Kim Novak, Otto Preminger, Max Von Sydow, Peter Sellers, François Truffaut, Fanny Ardant.

• *Diplomats, dignitaries and academics*: Former U.S. Ambassador to France, Walter Curley; U.S. Ambassador to the U.N., Joseph V. Reed; Cardinal John O'Connor, Archbishop of New York; Anthony Cardinal Bevilacqua, Archbishop of Philadelphia; Armand Hammer; Sarah Ferguson, Duchess of York; Professor Herbert Morris, Dean of Humanities at UCLA; Warren Keegan, Professor of Business at Pace University in New York; Professor Wesley Posvar, former President of the University of Pittsburgh.

• *Executives from the following corporations*: AT&T International, Coca-Cola, Proctor & Gamble, Chase Manhattan Bank, American Express, Merrill Lynch, New York Chamber of Commerce and Industry, Boeing Aircraft, General Electric, Westinghouse Electric, Bank of America, Max Factor, Rand Corporation, Bertlesmann Music Group-RCA, Veuve Cliquot Inc., McDonald's Corporation, Rover, British Aerospace.

What do his students say?

Academy® award winning director and actress, **Emma Thompson** (as quoted in the *Guardian*): 'The excitement of learning something new was overwhelming. Michel not only taught me Spanish, he opened my eyes to the possibilities of a completely different kind of learning. Michel forbids his students to practise, or to try to remember. Michel takes the burden off the student and upon himself… Learning Spanish with Michel was the most extraordinary learning experience of my life – it was unforgettable.'

New York film-maker **Woody Allen**, (as quoted in *USA Today* and *Business Life*): 'I am a poor student, particularly with languages. I had years of Spanish in school and could never speak a word… (but) learning with Michel: it's like a kid who loves baseball and who just knows every ball player, every batting average, every statistic about the game. They've learned it all effortlessly. It's the same with Michel. You learn a language effortlessly. It is amazing. (He)…had me speaking French and I learned it in a way I've never forgotten, and it was painless. A tremendous experience.'

Customer feedback

'I am writing to congratulate you on the highly original and successful language courses by Michel Thomas; I am currently working on German and French while my daughter, at my suggestion, has bought the Italian course.'

R Harris

'I have now finished the eight cassette Italian course and would like to say how pleased I am with it. I am a scientist, with all my neurones in the side of my brain that deals with understanding, and next to none on the side that deals with memory. This has meant my ability to retain vocabulary and learn a language has been about as bad as it comes. Against all odds, the Michel Thomas course has left me with a real sense of achievement, and a tremendous basis for further progress in learning Italian.'

T A Whittingham

Recording 1

Vamos a comenzar /	*We are going to start*
vamos a empezar	
comenzamos / empezamos	*we're going to start*
empecemos	*let's start*
Me gusta ...	*I like ...*
Me gusta estar aquí	*I like to be here*
Quiero hacerlo pero ...	*I want to do it but ...*
lo haré, lo hará *I will do it, he/she/ will do it*	
no lo haré, no voy a hacerlo	*I won't do it, I won't do it*
hoy porque ...	*today because*
... estoy muy ocupado	*... I'm very busy*
... estoy demasiado ocupado ...	*... I'm too busy*
... para hacerlo	*... to do it*
Tengo ganas de ...	*I feel like ...*
Tengo ganas de hacerlo	*I feel like doing it*
No tengo ganas de ir allí	*I don't feel like going there*
No tengo ganas de quedarme aquí	*I don't feel like staying here*
Tengo ganas de salir	*I feel like going out*
Me parece que ...	*It seems to me that, I think that ...*
creo que ..., pienso que ...	*I believe that ..., I think that ...*
Me parece que ella no tiene	*It seems to me that she doesn't*
ganas de ir allí	*feel like going there*
Estoy de acuerdo con usted	*I agree with you*
De acuerdo	*OK, agreed*
No estoy de acuerdo con él	*I don't agree with him*

7

¿Cuál es su opinión?	*What is your opinion?*
¿Cuál es tu opinión?	*What is your opinion?*
¿Qué piensa?	*What do you think?*
¿Qué piensas, Roberto?	
¿Qué piensan ustedes?	

Me interesa — *It interests me*

| Me interesa mucho, muchísimo | *It interests me a lot, very much* |
| Desafortunadamente no me interesa | *Unfortunately it doesn't interest me* |

Creo que ... — *I think that ...*

Creo que él va a estar allí ...	*I think that he will be there ...*
... esta tarde	*... this afternoon*
Es demasiado tarde para hacerlo	*It's too late to do it*

tarde *means 'late' as well as 'afternoon'*; es tarde *is 'it is late'*

| Creo que él va a estar aquí esta noche | *I think that he is going to be here tonight* |
| Veremos, vamos a ver | *We will see* |

No será posible ... — *It won't be possible ...*

| ... hacerlo así | *... to do it like this, in this way* |
| No lo creo | *I don't think so, I don't believe it* |

Seguro, seguramente — *sure, surely*
Claro — *Of course*

| Naturalmente | *Naturally* |
| Claro que estoy seguro | *Of course I'm sure* |

Mira / Mire ... — *Look ...*

... está sobre la mesa	*... it's on the table*
¿Puede ponerlo, podría ponerlo ...	*Will / Can you put it, could you put it ...*
... debajo de la mesa?	*... under the table?*

Es necesario ...	*It is necessary ...*
Tenemos que ...	*We have to ...*
Hay que ...	*One must ...*
... ir allí	*... to go there*
No es necesario / No	*It is not necessary to buy it ...*
hay que comprarlo ...	
... porque es muy caro	*... because it is very expensive*
Necesito, lo necesito	*I need, I need it*
No lo necesito ahora	*I don't need it now*
Es todo lo que necesito	*It is all I need*

Note the use of lo que *in the middle of the sentence (literally 'all what I need')*

Esto / Eso es todo lo que necesito	*This / That is all I need*
Es todo lo que quiero	*It is all I want*
¿Esto es todo lo que quiere?	*Is this all you want?*
Quiero algo más	*I want something else*
¿Necesita algo más?	*Do you need anything else?*
No gracias, esto es todo	*No thank you, that's all*
¿Puede mostrarme ...?	*Will you / Can you show me?*
Sí, voy a mostrarle, le muestro	*Yes, I'll show you*

PRESENT TENSE USED FOR FUTURE
mostrar *means 'to show'*
muestro *means 'I show, I'll show'; le muestro, 'I'll show you'*
The future is often expressed by the present tense in Spanish

¿Puede / podría decirme ...	*Will you / Can you / Could you tell me ...*
... a qué hora va a estar listo?	*... what time it is going to be ready?*
... a qué hora estará listo?	*... what time it will be ready ?*

Voy a informarme	*I will find out*
	(literally, inform myself)
Necesito cierta información	*I need certain information*
Tengo que informarme	*I have to find out*
Voy a decirle mañana, le diré mañana	*I will tell you tomorrow*

poder *means 'to be able'*; podré *I will be able*

No voy a poder, no podré ...	*I will not be able ...*
... hacerlo	*... to do it*
No podrá venir con nosotros	*He will not be able to come with us*
No va a poder venir con nosotros	*He isn't going to be able to come with us*

buscar *means 'to look for'*

Lo busco, lo estoy buscando ...	*I am looking for it ...*
... pero no puedo encontrarlo	*... but I can't find it*
¿Tiene algo para mí?	*Do you have something for me?*
No, no tengo nada	*No, I don't have anything,*
	I have nothing
Ya no tengo más	*I don't have it any longer, any more*
Hay un mensaje para usted	*There is a message for you*
Hay unos mensajes para usted	*There are some messages for you*
¿Hay mensajes para mí?	*Are there messages for me?*
¿Hay algún mensaje para mí?	*Is there any message for me?*
Sí, hay algunos	*Yes, there are some*
¿Cuánto es?	*How much is it?*
¿Cuánto es esto / eso?	*How much is this / that?*
¿Cuánto cuesta?	*How much does it cost?*
¿Cuál es el precio?	*What is the price?*
¿Cuánto vale?	*How much is it worth?*

| No vale mucho | It's not worth much |
| ¿Cuánto le debo? | How much do I owe you? |

---

debo *means 'I must, I'm supposed to, I should'*
¿Qué debo hacer? *is 'What should I do?'*
Debo salir *is 'I must go out'*

Está muy bien — It's fine, all right
Está bien así — It's OK like this

Me parece que / creo que ... — I think that ...
... va a decidir / decidirá hacerlo — ... he will decide to do it

Voy a hacerlo ... — I'm going to do it ...
... inmediatamente / ahora mismo — ... immediately / right now
... en seguida — ... right away
Quiero hacerlo — I want to do it
Me gustaría hacerlo — I would like to do it

---

me gusta *means 'I like'*, me gustaría *'I would like'*

Me gustaría saber ... — I would like to know ...
... a qué hora ... — ... at what time ...
... él puede / podrá / podría ... — ... he can / will be able to / could ...
... estar aquí — ... be here

---

olvidar *means 'to forget'*

No olvidaré / no voy a olvidar ... — I will not forget ...
... decirle / darle — ... to tell / to give you / him / her / them
... dárselo — ... to give it to you / him / her / them

Voy a dárselo a usted — I'm going to give it to you
Tengo ganas de hacerlo ... — I feel like doing it. ...
... pero no sé si puedo hacerlo ahora — ... but I don't know if I can do it now

11

No vale la pena ...   *It's not worth the trouble ...*
... ir allí   *... to go there / going there*

Podemos ir allí si quiere / si quieres   *We can go there if you want*
¿Quiere / quieres venir conmigo?   *Do you want to come with me?*
Me gustaría ir con usted / contigo   *I'd like to go with you*
¿Le gustaría / Te gustaría venir   *Would you like to come*
  conmigo?   *with me?*

Sí, claro que sí / ¿cómo no?   *Yes, of course*
Me gustaría mucho   *I'd like to very much*
Con mucho gusto   *With much pleasure*
Gracias por su gentileza   *That's nice of you*
De acuerdo / Vale   *Agreed, OK*
Esto / Eso me gusta   *This / That pleases me, I like it*
Es una buena idea   *It's a good idea*
Tiene razón   *You are right*
Tiene toda la razón   *You are quite right*
Tiene razón y estoy de acuerdo   *You are right and I agree*
  con usted   *with you*

Me gusta quedarme aquí ...   *I like to stay / staying here ...*
... porque estoy cansado   *... because I'm tired*
Me gusta descansar   *I like to rest*

Voy a descansar ...   *I'm going to rest ...*
... un poco / un rato   *... for a little / for a while*
... porque estoy muy cansado   *... because I'm very tired*

¿Vale la pena ir a verlo esta noche?	*Is it worth going to see it tonight?*
No, no vale la pena	*No, it's not worth it*

¡Es increíble!
It's incredible!

No lo creo	*I don't believe it*
Es increíble lo que me dice	*It's incredible what you're telling me*
Es magnífico / extraordinario	*It's great / magnificent / extraordinary*
Es excelente	*It's excellent*
Esto es muy interesante	*This is very interesting*

Me interesa mucho verlo	*It interests me a lot to see it*
Estoy muy interesado	*I am very interested*
Me interesa mucho ir a verlo	*I'm very interested to go and see it*
Ella es encantadora	*She is very charming, lovely, nice*
Me gusta mucho ir allí con usted	*I like very much to go there with you*

Lo siento
I'm sorry
Siento decirle ...
I'm sorry to tell you ...

... que no puedo ir a verlo	*... that I can't go to see it*
... con usted / contigo esta noche	*... with you tonight*
Siento decirle ...	*... I'm sorry to tell you ...*
... que no podría ir a verlo	*... that I wouldn't be able to go and see it*

... porque estoy muy ocupado	*... because I'm very busy*
... porque estaré, voy a estar muy ocupado	*... I shall be / I'm going to be very busy*

Tengo que hacerlo	*I have to do it*
Tendría que hacerlo	*I would have to do it*

Tiene que hacerlo	*He has to do it*
Tendría que hacerlo	*He would have to do it*
Tendríamos que ir allí	*We would have to go there*
Tendría que decirme	*You should tell me*
Debería hacerlo	*I should do it*
Debería esperarme	*You should wait for me*

Me gusta mucho / Me encanta viajar	*I like very much to travel*

de vacaciones *means 'on holiday'*

Creo que me voy de vacaciones ...	*I think I'm going on holiday ...*
... primero a España	*... first to Spain*
... y luego, más tarde a Italia	*... and then, later to Italy*
Me gustaría ...	*I would like ...*
... verle / ir a verle	*... to see him / to go and see him*
Creo que voy a salir pronto ...	*I think I'm going to leave soon ...*
... porque no puedo esperar	*... because I can't wait*
¿Cuándo cree que va a salir?	*When do you think you will leave?*
Pienso salir pronto	*I think I'll leave soon*
¿Cuándo piensa salir?	*When do you think you'll leave?*
Espero salir pronto	*I hope to leave soon*
¿Cuánto tiempo piensa ...	*How long do you think ...*
... quedarse en Madrid?	*... you'll stay in Madrid?*
Pienso quedarme una semana en España	*I think I'll stay a week in Spain*

Tengo ganas de ...	*I feel like ...*
... ir al cine esta noche	*... going to the cinema tonight*
... para ver una película	*... (in order) to see a film, a picture*

una película interesante	*an interesting picture*
Ella no tiene ganas de ir allí	*She doesn't feel like going there ...*
... esta noche, quizás mañana	*... tonight, perhaps tomorrow*
Pienso salir / irme ...	*I think I'll leave / go away ...*
... la semana que viene	*... next week*
... el mes que viene	*... next month*
... o en dos semanas	*... or in two weeks*
Quiero tenerlo	*I want to have it*
Voy a comprarlo	*I'm going to buy it*
No voy a comprarlo porque ...	*I'm not going to buy it because ...*
... es demasiado caro	*... it's too expensive*
... es muy caro	*... it's very expensive*
No pienso comprarlo	*I don't plan to buy it*

pensar *'to think' is used for planning*
esperar *'to hope' also means 'to expect'*

No tengo la intención de   *I don't intend to buy it*
comprarlo

PRONUNCIATION OF LETTER 'c'
The letter 'c' *followed by* 'i' *or* 'e' *is pronounced* 'th' *in Castilian Spanish but* 's' *in other parts of the Spanish-speaking world. But before* 'a', 'o', 'u' *it is always* 'k'.
You'll hear 'intenthión' *in Castilian Spanish, but* 'intensión' *in many other parts of Spain and in Latin America. Another example:* 'Barthelona' *and* 'Barselona'.

No tengo la intención de hacerlo — *I don't intend to do it*

Pienso ir allí con usted	*I plan to go there with you*
Espero ir allí con usted	*I expect / I hope to go there with you*
Voy a tomarlo	*I'm going to take it*
Va a estar listo pronto	*It will be ready soon*

¿A qué hora ...	*At what time ...*
... va a estar aquí?	*... are you going to be here?*
No tengo tiempo de hacerlo	*I don't have time to do it*
No tiene tiempo de hacerlo	*He doesn't have time to do it*
No tenemos tiempo de hacerlo	*We don't have time to do it*
¿Cuánto tiempo tiene?	*How much time do you have?*
No sé cuándo ...	*I don't know when ...*
... va a estar / estará listo	*... it will be ready*
Creo que ...	*I think ...*
... va a estar / estará listo pronto	*... it will be ready soon*

¿Debo abrir la ventana?	*Should I open the window?*
¿Abro la ventana?	*Shall I open the window?*
Cierro la puerta	*I'm closing the door*
¿Cierro la puerta?	*Shall I close the door?*

All you have to do to change a statement (I'm closing the door) into a question (Shall I close the door?) is to make it sound like a question, with the right inflexion in your voice. The order of the words doesn't change.
In written Spanish you put a question mark ¿ at the beginning as well as ? at the end of the question.

Le espero	*I'm waiting for you*
¿Le espero?	*Shall I wait for you?*
¿Le acompaño?	*Shall I accompany you?*
¿Voy / vengo con usted?	*Shall I go / come with you?*
Le llamo más tarde / mañana	*I'll call you later / tomorrow*
¿Le llamo más tarde?	*Shall I call you later?*
Salimos	*We are leaving*
¿Salimos?	*Shall we leave?*
Vamos a hacerlo	*We are going to do it*
¿Qué vamos a hacer?	*What shall we do?*
Yo sé que no va a poder hacerlo	*I know he won't be able to do it*
Tengo que ir a verlo	*I have to go and see it*
Voy a ir a verlo	*I am going to see it*
Iba a verlo	*He was going to see it*
Iba a hacerlo	*I was going to do it*
No iba a hacerlo	*He wasn't going to do it*
No iba a decirle ...	*I wasn't going to tell you ...*
... que iba a hacerlo para usted	*... that I was going to do it for you*
Iba a comprarlo	*I was going to buy it*
No iba a encontrarlo	*I wasn't going to find it*

Él iba a estar aquí esta mañana	*He was going to be here this afternoon*
No iba a esperar	*I wasn't going to wait*
No iba a esperarle	*I wasn't going to wait for you*

Sé, lo sé, no lo sé — *I know, I know it, I don't know it*

No sé dónde está	*I don't know where it is*
No puedo encontrarlo	*I can't find it*
¿Puede decirme dónde está?	*Can you tell me where it is?*
¿Podría decirme?	*Could you / would you be able to tell me?*
Tengo que saberlo	*I have to know (it)*

saber *means 'to know'*
sé *means 'I know'*; sabe, *'he/she knows', 'you know'*; sabes *'you know' (informal)*; saben *'you know', 'they know'*

¿Qué sabe? — *What do you know?*

| ¿Por qué no lo sabes? | *Why don't you know (it)? (to a friend)* |

Nadie sabe dónde está — *Nobody knows where it is*

| Nadie puede encontrarlo | *Nobody can find it* |

sabía *means 'I knew', ' he/she knew', 'you knew'*; sabías *is 'you knew' (informal)*; sabían *'you knew', 'they knew'*

Lo sabía — *I knew (it)*
No lo sabía — *I didn't know (it)*

No sabía que usted iba a estar aquí	*I didn't know you were going to be here*
No iba a decirle ...	*I wasn't going to tell you ...*
... que iba a comprarlo para usted	*... that I was going to buy it for you*

llegar *means 'to arrive'*

No sabía que ...	*I didn't know ...*
... iba a llegar hoy	*... you were going to arrive today*
Yo sabía que todo iba a estar listo	*I knew everything was going to be ready*
Sé que nunca ...	*I know that I never ...*
... voy a poder / podré hacerlo así	*... will be able to do it that way*

Recording 2

¿Qué hay?   *What is there?*

¿Qué hay? can also mean 'What's up?', 'What's the matter?', 'What's going on?'

¿Qué hay para comer?   *What is there to eat?*
¿Qué hay para beber?   *What is there to drink?*

ofrecer *means 'to offer'*

¿Puedo ofrecerle algo ...   *Can I offer you something ...*
... para beber?   *... to drink?*
Sí, pero primero tengo que ...   *Yes, but first I have to ...*
... hacer una llamada telefónica   *... make a phone call*
... llamar por teléfono   *... telephone*
Y después, voy a salir   *And afterwards I'm going to leave*

PRONUNCIATION OF THE LETTER 'Z'
The letter 'z' is always 'th' in Castilian and 's' elsewhere

la primera vez   *the first time*
la segunda vez   *the second time*
la tercera vez   *the third time*
la próxima vez   *the next time*
dos veces   *two times, twice*
muchas veces   *many times*
Voy a hacerlo muchas veces   *I'm going to do it many times*

No tengo ganas de hacerlo   *I don't feel like doing it*
No tengo ganas de ir allí solo   *I don't feel like going there alone*
Voy a hacerlo   *I'm going to do it*

21

Iba a hacerlo	*I was going to do it*
No sabía que iba a estar aquí	*I didn't know you were going to be here*

Yo no sabía que **usted** iba a estar aquí	*I didn't know you were going to be here*
Él no sabía que **ella** iba a estar aquí	*He didn't know she was going to be here*
No sabía que iba a salir ...	*I didn't know you were going to leave ...*
... esta tarde	*... this afternoon*
Vamos a empezar ...	*We are going to start ...*
... pronto / en seguida	*... soon / right away*
... inmediatamente	*... immediately*
Voy a esperar	*I'm going to wait*
Iba a esperar	*He was going to wait*
No iba a esperar	*He wasn't going to wait*
No sabía ...	*I didn't know ...*
... que iba a estar aquí ...	*... that you were going to be here ...*
... hoy / esta mañana	*... today / this morning*
No sabía ...	*I didn't know*
... que iban a estar aquí	*... that you were (all) going to be here*

Generalmente ...	*Generally / usually ...*

... no lo hago así   *... I don't do it that way*

SPECIAL = ESPECIAL

Words beginning sp-, st- or sc- in English usually start esp-, est- *or* esc- *in Spanish: 'Spain' is* España; *'student'* estudiante; *'school'* escuela.

ENGLISH WORDS ENDING '-TY'

Words ending in -ty *usually end in* -tad *or* -dad *in Spanish:*
especialidad; libertad; oportunidad; cualidad

Generalmente no me gusta hacerlo   *Generally I don't like doing it*
Generalmente no voy allí   *Generally I don't go there*
A menudo   *Often*
Frecuentemente   *Frequently*
Casi nunca voy allí   *I almost never go there*

---

acabar *means 'to finish'*
acabo de + *infinitive (to have just ...) is an easy way of expressing the past tense!*

Acabo de ...   *I have just ...*
Acabo de verlo   *I have just seen it*
Acaba de salir   *He has just left*
Acabo de llegar ...   *I have just arrived ...*
... hace dos días   *... two days ago*
Acaba de llamarme ...   *He has just called me ...*
... hace diez minutos   *... ten minutes ago*
Ella acaba de salir / de irse   *She has just gone out / left*
Acabo de decirle   *I have just told you*
Acabo de comprarlo   *I have just bought it*
Acabo de hablar con él   *I have just spoken to him*
Acaba de decirme   *He has just told me*

23

Voy a volver / Volveré ...   *I'll come back ...*
... en seguida / pronto   *... right away / soon*
Va a volver / Volverá ...   *She will come back ...*
... muy pronto / más tarde   *... very soon / later*
Acaba de salir hace diez minutos ...   *She has just left ten minutes ago ...*
... y va a volver / volverá más tarde   *... and she'll come back later*

No tengo ganas de salir ahora ...   *I don't feel like going out now ...*
... porque estoy muy   *... because I'm very tired*
   cansado / cansada

preferir *means 'to prefer';* prefiero *'I would rather ...'*

Prefiero ...   *I would rather / I would prefer to ...*
... quedarme aquí   *... stay here*

Acaba de comprar un libro ...   *I have just bought a book ...*
... que encuentro muy interesante   *... that I find very interesting*
Lo encuentro muy interesante   *I find it very interesting*
Creo que es muy interesante   *I think it is very interesting*

Hace diez minutos **que le espero** *I have been waiting ten minutes*
                                            for you

To say how long you have been waiting, doing something, working etc.
use hace (*literally 'it makes'*) + que + *the present tense.*

¿Cuánto tiempo hace que ...   *How long ...*
... está aquí en Madrid?   *... have you been here in Madrid?*

Quisiera / Me gustaría / Quiero   *I would like ...*
... hablar con él   *... to talk to him*
... verlo   *... to see it*

No está allí	*He isn't in / isn't there*
¿A qué hora va a estar / estará aquí?	*What time will he be here?*
¿Sabe a qué hora ...	*Do you know what time ...*
... va a llegar / llegará / llega?	*... he will arrive?*
... va a volver / volverá / vuelve?	*... he will come back / return?*
Puede / podría decirme ...	*Can / Could you tell me ...*
... a qué hora estará / va a estar aquí?	*... what time he will be here?*

> irse *means 'to leave', 'to go away'*
> dejar *means 'to leave (behind)' and also 'to let' (someone do something)*

dejar la llave	*to leave the key*
dejar un mensaje	*to leave a message*
¿Puede dejarme trabajar?	*Can you let me work?*
Me gustaría dejar un mensaje	*I'd like to leave a message*
¿Puedo dejar un mensaje?	*Can I leave a message?*
¿Puedo dejarle un mensaje?	*Can I leave you a message?*
¿Puede / Podría decirme ...	*Can / Could you tell me ...?*
¿Puede / Podría decirle ...	*Can / Could you tell him ...*
... que le llamaré más tarde?	*... that I'll call him later?*
... que le llamaré mañana?	*... that I'll call him tomorrow?*
... que le llamaré la semana que viene?	*... that I'll call him next week?*

la próxima vez　　　　　　　　*next time*

> THREE WORDS FOR 'TIME'
> vez *has the sense of one of a number of occasions*
> tiempo *is the general word for a period or passing of time*
> hora *is the point of time marked on a clock*

| una vez, dos veces | *once, twice* |
| tres, cuatro, cinco veces | *three, four, five times* |

seis, siete, ocho veces	*six, seven, eight times*
nueve, diez veces	*nine, ten times*
once, doce, trece veces	*eleven, twelve, thirteen times*
catorce, quince veces	*fourteen, fifteen times*
la primera vez	*the first time*
Es la última vez	*It's the last time*

expresar *means 'to express',* expresarse *'to express oneself'*

No sé cómo expresarlo exactamente ...	I don't know how to express it exactly ...

exacto *(exact) becomes* exactamente *(exactly).*
The 'o' *changes to* 'a' *before adding* '-mente'
Another example: seguro *becomes* seguramente

No sé cómo decirlo exactamente ...	*I don't know how to say it exactly ...*
... en español	*... in Spanish*
¿Cómo lo dice en español?	*How do you say it in Spanish?*
¿Cómo se dice en español?	*How does one say it in Spanish?*

SPECIAL USE OF 'SE'
Se *is frequently used to mean 'one' or 'you' , or to say something* '*is done*'

Se habla español aquí	*One speaks Spanish*
	Spanish is spoken here

escribir *means 'to write'*

le escribo	*I write to you*
Me escribe a menudo	*He writes to me often*
... frecuentemente	*... frequently*
¿Cómo se escribe?	*How do you write it / spell it?*
¿Puede escribirlo?	*Can you write it down?*

Escríbalo, por favor	*Write it down, please*
Se puede ...	*One can / It is possible / allowed ...*
¿Se puede entrar aquí?	*Can one come in?*
¿Se puede hacerlo?	*Can one do it?*
¿Se puede pasar?	*Can one pass / come in?*
¿Dónde se puede encontrarlo?	*Where can one find it?*

¿Está seguro de esto?	*Are you sure about this?*
absolutamente / totalmente	*absolutely / totally*
Sí, estoy absolutamente seguro	*Yes, I'm absolutely sure*

Note that you say seguro if you a man, segura if you are a woman

Lo sé porque ...	*I know because ...*
... acabo de leerlo ...	*... I've just read it ...*
... en el periódico	*... in the newspaper*
... en el periódico de hoy	*... in today's newspaper*

¿Puede / Podría decirme dónde ...	*Can / Could you tell me where ...*
... puedo encontrar un buen restaurante?	*... I can find a good restaurant?*
no muy lejos de aquí	*not very far from here*
Está muy lejos	*It's very far, a long way*
¿Está lejos de aquí?	*Is it far from here?*
No, no está lejos de aquí	*No, it's not far from here*
Está cerca de aquí	*It's near here*
Puede ir a pie	*You can walk*
¿Puedo ir a pie?	*Can I walk?*
Se puede ir a pie	*One can walk*
Necesito un coche	*I need a car*

In Spain a car is un coche, but in Mexico it's un carro

| ... para ir al restaurante | *... to go to the restaurant* |

27

'To rent a car' in Spain is alquilar un coche *but in Mexico it's* rentar un carro

Quisiera alquilar un coche	*I'd like to hire a car*
¿Dónde puedo alquilar un coche?	*Where can I hire a car?*
¿Cuánto es por día?	*How much is it per day?*
¿Cuánto cuesta ...	*How much does it cost ...*
... por semana?	*... per week?*
... por mes?	*... per month?*

¿dónde? *asks where someone or something is;* ¿a dónde? *asks where someone is going*
¿Dónde está? *but* ¿A dónde va?

¿Puede / Podría decirme ...	*Can you / Could you tell me ...*
... a dónde ir ...	*... where to go ...*
... para encontrar lo que quiero?	*... to find what I want?*
... para encontrar lo que busco?	*... to find what I'm looking for?*
Me gustaría / Quisiera saber ...	*I would like to know ...*
... lo que tengo que hacer ...	*... what I have to do ...*
... para obtener lo que quiero	*... to get what I want*
... para obtener lo que busco	*... to get what I'm looking for*

hay que *means 'one has to'*

Quiero saber ...	*I want to know ...*
... lo que hay que hacer ...	*... what one has to do ...*
... para obtenerlo	*... in order to obtain it*
Me gustaría saber ...	*I would like to know ...*
... a dónde hay que ir ...	*... where one has to go ...*
... para obtenerlo / encontrarlo	*... to have it / to find it*
... para comprarlo	*... to buy it*

¿Puede darme una explicación? *Can you give me an explanation?*

explicar *means 'to explain'*; una explicación *is 'an explanation'*
This is an exception to the rule that most English words ending in
'-ation' are identical in Spanish, with the ending '-ación'.
However, remember that most do obey this rule: información,
preparación, reservación, *etc.*
It's also worth noting that the verbs associated with these nouns are all
-ar *verbs :* informar, preparar, reservar

¿Puede explicarme dónde está?	*Can you tell me where it is?*
Gracias	*Thank you*
Le agradezco mucho	*I thank you very much*
Realmente le agradezco mucho	*I really do thank you very much*

Estoy enojado / enojada	*I'm angry, annoyed*
Estoy muy enojado / enojada	*I'm very angry, annoyed*

In Spain you'll often hear: Estoy enfadado / enfadada, *which also means 'I'm annoyed, angry'*

Estoy furioso / furiosa	*I'm furious*
Me preocupa	*I'm worried (literally, it preoccupies me)*
Me preocupa mucho	*I'm very worried*
Me preocupa ver esto	*I'm worried about seeing this*
No me preocupa	*I'm not worried*
Estoy aburrido / aburrida	*I'm bored*
Estoy muy aburrido	*I'm very bored*
¿Está aburrido?	*Are you bored?*
No me gusta estar aburrido	*I don't like being bored*
Creo que ... / Me parece que ...	*I think ...*

... todo está bien	*... everything is all right*
Voy a verlo una vez	*I'm going to see it once*
Voy a ir a verlo	*I'm going to go and see it*
No lo veo a menudo	*I don't see it often*
Por lo menos ...	*At least ...*

menos *means 'less'*; más o menos *means 'more or less'*

... lo veré / voy a verlo una vez	*... I'll see it once*

temprano *means 'early'*

¿Puede / puedes / pueden venir ...	*Can you come ...*
... un poco más temprano?	*... a little earlier?*

lleno *means 'full'*; llenar *is 'to fill up'*

Está muy lleno	*It's very full*
¿Puede llenarlo?	*Can you fill it up?*

limpio *is 'clean'*; sucio *is 'dirty'*

No está muy limpio	*It's not very clean*
Está sucio	*It's dirty*
Es perfecto	*It's perfect*
Perfectamente	*Perfectly*

calor *is 'heat'*; frío *is 'cold'*
For hot weather you say hace calor *(literally 'it makes heat')*
But a hot person says tengo calor *(literally 'I have heat')*

No me gusta el calor	*I don't like the heat*
Hace calor / frío hoy	*It's hot / cold (weather)*
Tengo calor / frío	*I'm hot / cold*
¿Tiene frío?	*Are you cold?*
No puedo soportar el calor	*I can't stand the heat*

Tengo hambre   *I'm hungry*
Tengo que comer algo ...   *I have to eat something ...*
... porque tengo hambre   *... because I'm hungry*
Tengo sed   *I'm thirsty*
Tengo que beber algo ...   *I have to drink something ...*
... porque tengo sed   *... because I'm thirsty*

Pienso / Creo que puedo hacerlo ... *I think I can do it ...*
... yo mismo   *... myself*

mismo *means 'self' and also 'same'; la misma cosa is 'the same thing';*
lo mismo *is 'the same'*

Quiero lo mismo   *I want the same*
Voy a tomar lo mismo   *I'm going to take / have the same*
No es lo mismo   *It's not the same*

Estoy (muy) sorprendido   *I'm (very) surprised*
Me sorprende   *It surprises me*
No me sorprende   *It doesn't surprise me*
Esto / Eso no me sorprende   *This / That doesn't surprise me*

traer *means 'to bring'; dar 'to give'; mostrar 'to show'*

¿Puede traerme algo?   *Can / Will you bring me something?*
¿Puede darme algo?   *Can you give me something?*
¿Puede mostrarme algo?   *Can you show me something?*
¿Puede mostrármelo?   *Can you show it to me?*

*Note that the personal me (me) comes before the object lo (it) and
that they are joined together at the end of the infinitive*

¿Puede traérmelo?   *Can you bring it to me?*
¿Cuándo puede traérmelo ... ?   *When can you bring it to me ...?*
... porque lo necesito y ...   *... because I need it and ...*
... tengo que tenerlo   *... I have to have it*

vivir *is 'to live'*

¿Dónde vive / vives / viven?   *Where do you live?*
¿Usted vive aquí?   *Do you live here?*

saber *is 'to know' in the sense of knowing a fact or some general knowledge:*
conocer *is 'to know' in the sense of being acquainted with somebody or something*

Sabe donde está   *He knows where it is*
Conozco ...   *I know ...*
... la ciudad / el país   *... the city / the country*

PERSONAL 'A'
Conocer a ... *is used for 'to know a person'. Whenever the object of a verb is a person, not a thing, you always insert 'a' between the verb and the person*

Voy a llamarle   *I'm going to call / phone him*
Voy a **llamar a** mi amigo   *I'm going to call / phone my friend*

querer *means 'to want' and also 'to love'*

Lo quiere   *He wants it*
Él **quiere a** su amiga   *He loves his girlfriend*
Conozco la ciudad   *I know the city*
Conozco a esta señora   *I know this lady*
No conozco Madrid   *I don't know Madrid*

No conozco a nadie	*I don't know anybody*
¿Conoce esta ciudad?	*Do you know this city?*
¿**Conoce a** esta señora?	*Do you know this lady?*
¿Sabe dónde está?	*Do you know where it is?*
Mi amigo viene aquí ...	*My friend comes here ...*
... todos los días	*... every day*
Suele venir aquí	*He usually comes here*
Suele hacerlo ...	*He usually does it ...*
... casi todos los días	*... almost every day*

quizás, quizá *means 'perhaps', 'maybe'*

Quizás no le gusta ...	*Perhaps you don't like ...*
Quizá no le gustaría ...	*Perhaps you wouldn't like ...*
... quedarse aquí	*... to stay here ...*
... porque hay mucha gente	*... because there are many people*

la gente *is 'people'*; tanto / tanta *means 'so much', 'so many'*

Hay tanta gente aquí	*There are so many people here*
Por mi parte ...	*For my part ...*
... no voy a quedarme aquí ahora	*... I'm not going to stay here now*
Hay mucho ruido	*There's a lot of noise*

hay *is 'there is', 'there are'*; había *'there was', 'there were'*;
habrá *'there will be'*

Había mucha gente aquí ayer	*There were many people here yesterday*
Habrá mucha gente	*There will be many people*
Había demasiado ruido	*There was too much noise*
Habrá mucho ruido	*There will be a lot of noise*

Habrá **mucho más** ruido ... | *There will be much more noise ...*
Habrá **mucho menos** ruido ... | *There will be much less noise ...*
... aquí mañana | *... here tomorrow*

Espero tener ... | *I hope to have ...*
Espero que voy a tener ... | *I hope I'll have ...*
... la oportunidad / la ocasión ... | *... the opportunity ...*
... de verlo | *... of seeing it*
Espero tener la ocasión ... | *I hope to have the opportunity ...*
... de ver **a** mis amigos | *... to see my friends*
... de visitar **a** mis amigos | *... to visit my friends*

Note the use of the personal 'a' again

Voy a llamar **a** mi amigo ... | *I'm going to phone my friend ...*
... para saber si puede venir ... | *... to find out if he can come ...*
... con nosotros | *... with us*

vemos *means 'we see'*;
nos vemos *'we see each other' , 'we meet'*

¿A qué hora nos vemos | *What time shall we meet*
   mañana? | *tomorrow?*
A la misma hora | *At the same time*
A las diez | *At ten o'clock*
Vamos a vernos / nos veremos ... | *We will meet ...*
Nos vemos ... | *We'll meet ...*
... mañana a la misma hora | *... tomorrow at the same time*

Ahora puedo hacerme entender ... | *Now I can make myself understood ...*
... en español | *... in Spanish*
Me parece que es suficiente | *I think that's enough*
¡Buena suerte! | *Good luck!*

34

Le deseo buena suerte
Adiós, hasta luego
¡Buen viaje!

I wish you good luck
Goodbye, until soon / until later
Have a good journey!

The Michel Thomas Language Range

8-hour Language Courses*

These all-audio courses provide an accelerated method for learning that is truly revolutionary. In just a few hours, anyone can gain a functional working knowledge of a language, without books, note-taking or conscious memorising.

*The first 2 hours of the 8-hour course are also available separately – see order form opposite for details.

Language Builders

The perfect follow-on to the 8-hour course. In 2 hours, you will increase your word power and gain extra confidence in your pronunciation. With a full listing of all the crucial words and phrases, you will able to improve your spelling, reading and writing too.

If you would like to find out more, please get in touch with us

For general enquiries:
Call: 020 7873 6261   Fax: 020 7873 6299
Email: michelthomas-enquiries@hodder.co.uk

To place an order, please fill in the order form on the next page and send it to the FREEPOST address listed, or:
Call: 01235 400414   Fax: 01235 400454
Email: orders@bookpoint.co.uk

You can write to us at: Hodder & Stoughton Educational, 338 Euston Road, London NW1 3BH

Visit our website at: www.madaboutbooks.com

MICHEL THOMAS ORDER FORM

Please complete and send back to us at the FREEPOST address listed below.

2-hour course CD £14.99

French	ISBN 0 340 78064 9	☐
German	ISBN 0 340 78066 5	☐
Italian	ISBN 0 340 78070 3	☐
Spanish	ISBN 0 340 78068 1	☐

2-hour course cassette £14.99

French	ISBN 0 340 77550 5	☐
German	ISBN 0 340 77551 3	☐
Italian	ISBN 0 340 77553 X	☐
Spanish	ISBN 0 340 77552 1	☐

8-hour course CD £70

French	ISBN 0 340 78063 0	☐
German	ISBN 0 340 78065 7	☐
Italian	ISBN 0 340 78069 X	☐
Spanish	ISBN 0 340 78067 3	☐

8-hour course cassette £70

French	ISBN 0 340 77554 8	☐
German	ISBN 0 340 77555 6	☐
Italian	ISBN 0 340 77557 2	☐
Spanish	ISBN 0 340 77556 4	☐

Language Builder CD £20

French	ISBN 0 340 78969 7	☐
German	ISBN 0 340 78973 5	☐
Italian	ISBN 0 340 78975 1	☐
Spanish	ISBN 0 340 78971 9	☐

Language Builder Cassette £20

French	ISBN 0 340 78968 9	☐
German	ISBN 0 340 78972 7	☐
Italian	ISBN 0 340 78974 3	☐
Spanish	ISBN 0 340 78970 0	☐

Title_____ Initials _____ Surname _____

Delivery Address _____

_____

_____ Postcode _____

Telephone _____

Methods of payment: Cash ☐ Cheque ☐ Credit Card ☐ Debit Card ☐
Please make cheques payable to Bookpoint Ltd
Card Number ☐☐☐☐ ☐☐☐☐ ☐☐☐☐ ☐☐☐☐
Expiry Details ☐☐/☐☐ Issue Number (Switch & Delta only) ☐
For orders under £20 please add £2.00 for p&p

Signature _____ **Total £** _____
Cardholder's Address (if different from above) _____

_____

Please send your completed order form to: **Michel Thomas Language Courses, Hodder & Stoughton Educational, FREEPOST NW6148, 338 Euston Road, London NW1 3YS**